AFTERMATH

AFTERMATH

BY

MARTINE ASHLEY

First Edition: September 2020
Printed in the United States of America
ISBN: [9781648586453]

This is for every soul that's battling silently. I hope my words not only reach you but give you a sense of hope. I also hope you know how enough you are right now in this very moment.

Welcome to Aftermath.

The Aftermath you're faced with after making it Through Your Storm is one of the most destructive scenes you'll ever witness. You've withstood the rain (loss), the hail (heartbreak), the winds (pain), and all the chaos (trauma) that arrives along with a storm. Amid all the carnage and damage afterward you're left in fear wondering what's next. It's terrifying but relieving all simultaneously. Yes, what's next is scary, but the fact that you made it through everything that was meant to destroy you brings this sense of relief. You prevailed with all of your doubts and fears staring you dead in your eyes. You tackled reliving traumatic experiences, accountability, responsibility, forgiveness, and healing. There's beauty you don't even recognize standing right in front of you. You've removed all the dead weight and now there's finally room for growth. You've created endless possibilities for happiness and peace. It all comes together, and you've finally found your little piece of paradise.

Walking Away.

It's never as easy as getting up and walking away.
But then it is.
See, I look back to the beginning of this hell, and I ask myself a million times,
"Why didn't you get up and walk away before it got this bad?"
Then I remember there were countless times I not only thought about it, but I was prepared to do so and then his smile would cross my mind.
When his smile crossed my mind, so would his laugh.
When his laugh crossed my mind, so would his touch.
When his touch crossed my mind, so would the amazing memories we shared.
And when the memories we shared crossed my mind, I felt guilty for wanting to leave because of the things he lacked.
When I felt guilty for wanting to leave, I beat myself.
'I mean, what made me feel so special that I could judge and then leave someone for what they lacked not knowing where it stemmed from, or the trauma they endured that explains why they lacked what they lacked?'
As I was beating myself up, I created countless excuses for him and his actions.
'Maybe no one took the time to be patient and love him. Maybe everyone gave up on him too soon. Maybe, just maybe I'm the one he needs to get past this.'
After processing all of those things through my mind, one thing remained clear throughout the midst of the chaos.
I loved this man beyond words could ever explain.
And for a very long time, that was enough for me, that was enough for us, and that was enough to stay.
Until one day, it wasn't.
It's never as easy as getting up and walking away,
But maybe it should be.
Especially when it costs you, yourself. It should be easy.

REMINDER.
We are not owed closure,
And we don't always receive the closure we deserve,
But we do get the things people elected to say.
We do get the way they've made us feel.
We get the choices people make,
And sometimes that's as close to closure as we get.
And that's all we need to move forward.

- Martine Ashley

You deserve…

It's discouraging.
When you love someone, who doesn't love you back.
When you fight so hard to keep a relationship alive just for it to fail in the end.
Failing in love and getting your heart broken on countless occasions can take a toll on you.
I know in all that pain, it's hard to raise your head and grant your mind permission to consider the positives you've been presented with,
But I want you to truly comprehend what this heartbreak has allowed you to see.
Look at the great fight you put up to make that toxic relationship work.
It's killing you and draining you in every way possible and you simply fight harder.
You've got this immense amount of will and strength to keep fighting despite how often you've been kicked down or pushed away.
Now imagine utilizing all of that strength for you.
Fighting for you, protecting you, pushing yourself to be the best version of you yet.
We can only fight for people for so long, but we can fight for ourselves forever.
You deserve to experience the love and the energy you provide everyone else.
Now you can give yourself that.

- Martine Ashley

People have so many misconceptions about toxic relationships. People speculate that the signs are so easily detectable. People assume that it's as easy as getting up and walking away once you've been sucked in for so long. The truth is many of us who've been in toxic relationships never realize we're in one till it's at the highest toxicity. There are so many signs we neglect to see, or we overlook because we never thought it would be us. We never believe these small signs could ever lead us into a toxic relationship that destroys us.

I never knew.
Until now.

The Signs I Missed

I was fortunate enough to go through it, make it out, become stronger and tell **my story**.

INVALIDATION.

Anytime I'd feel something other than happiness, or we'd discuss our past, I'd get responses like,
"At least it's not like what I had to go through."
"You're doing too much."
"Nothing you go through could ever compare to what I've gone through."
"I guarantee I went through worse than you."
"Damn really? That's bad… It still doesn't compare to my struggles."

Anytime I felt something that differed from what he thought I should feel was invalidated immediately.
"You shouldn't feel like that."
"You don't have the right to feel like that."
"You're taking this too seriously."
"You shouldn't even be upset about that."

I had never felt smaller or like I didn't matter than when I was with him. It takes a toll on you. You feel like you're going crazy, especially when you're always there for them, validating them, and creating a safe place for them to feel comfortable enough to display their feelings. All you want is the same respect, the same care, and the same comfort.

After someone dismisses you long enough, you establish in your mind that no one gives a damn about how you feel, what you've gone through, or what you have to say. You feel so unimportant. You feel like your words mean nothing.

From that point forward, I decided never to speak about how I feel again. I mean, what's the point? Why does it matter? It's not like anyone cares anyway, right?

It wasn't until I finally removed myself from that situation, I realized invalidation is a form of emotional abuse.

Can you invalidate someone's feelings unintentionally? Absolutely. I also believe that if someone can dictate who or what's worthy of sympathy but feel they're owed all the sympathy in the world, it's intentional.

It sucks because still to this day, I sometimes struggle with opening up. After all, I don't ever want my feelings to be disregarded again. I never want to second guess if I'm overreacting by having feelings that are normal to have. I'm still healing, and I'm still learning.

I've learned that you may feel how you feel.
I've learned that no one may tell you that your feelings don't matter.
I've learned that no one in this world is worth going through emotional abuse for.

Everyone has had their fair share of struggles, trauma, and battling demons. We've all suffered and just because you feel you "had it worse" or because you don't understand one's pain doesn't mean you get to dictate when people should feel or if they should feel.

The most dangerous people are insecure people who don't want to repair their wounds but would rather inflict wounds onto innocent people. They utilize their trauma, their pain, and their wounds to force people to feel as insignificant as they do on the inside.

- Martine Ashley

INSECURITIES

I had never witnessed a man go out of his way to make me, the girl he's supposed to love, feel so bad, and uplift him. It was like he found strength and security in trying to break me down. It made him happy to destroy me.

"You know you stay downgrading after me, But I keep on upgrading after you."
I was hanging out with friends; he pulls me aside and tells me that. This comes after I've accepted the fact that he just doesn't care about me, so I put my focus into moving on after years of waiting for him to get it together. It was so random and unexpected.
He walked away with such pride and happiness while I was left stuck, broken and confused.
Why would someone go out of their way unprovoked to hurt someone they claimed once upon a time to love?

He was so easily influenced by peer pressure from his boys it was scary. All his beliefs and morals went straight out the window if his boys had other plans in mind, even at the expense of me. He could never stand on his own two feet. It got so bad he even had sex to prove to his boys he "got it like that." Mind you, he was a virgin who expressed to me many times that he wanted to lose it to someone special. Come to discover he didn't even know the name of the girl he slept with. He got so drunk to just get it over with. "I had to get my street cred up!" Is what he told me when I asked him about it—a man throwing his morals out the window to prove a point to bunch of other men.

He hated that I didn't need to rely on him and that I was doing huge, amazing things on my own. Women are becoming breadwinners.

Women are securing their bag and needing a man to lean financially on isn't a priority or requirement anymore. He despised that I was 'GETTIN IT!' I had multiple streams of income. I was working on numerous projects. My book *Through The Storm* was reaching success higher than I ever imagined. So, someone who cares about you should be ecstatic that you're doing the damn thing, right? Nope. It was like the more success I gained, the angrier he got, the more insecure he got, and the more he changed. He held it against me every chance he got. Imagine doing something you love, having all the success in the world with it just to have the person you care about most make it seem so miniature.

He let his insecurities get the best of him. He not only let his insecurities ruin him, but he took all of that anger out onto me.

DIMMING MY LIGHT

Anything that concerned celebrating me or building me up, he was always against expressing his congratulations towards me. He could never even compliment me either. When I look back, I can't remember a time where he called me beautiful or told me I looked nice. It's like he just never wanted me to feel good about myself.

I remember selling 1000 copies of my first ever book, and I was so proud of myself. I put myself out there, people resonated, and people were enjoying the book I put my heart and soul into. I've learned that it's so important to celebrate yourself, so I did just that. I posted on Instagram of how proud of myself I was and just like he always does, he made me feel small and unimportant.

"You sold 1000 copies of your book?"
"OMG Yes, I did, I still can't believe I did."
"Oh, I mean, I guess that's alright."

Or he'd use the expression, "I'm not going to big your head up." For those not familiar with this phrase, it means he will not compliment me because he doesn't want me to think too highly of myself. He doesn't want me to get too "cocky."

Do you know the worst part of dealing with men like this? It's watching him freely and happily have no issue with complimenting, uplifting or supporting his boys, his friends that were girls, and damn near everyone else in the world except for me. It creates this heavyweight in your chest, and you question if it's you. Am I just not good enough? Am I not pretty enough? Is there something wrong with me?

No feeling compares to loving someone so much that instead of coming to terms with the fact they just don't love you back the same you'd rather look in the mirror picking at yourself trying to figure out what you need to do to keep this person from walking out of your life.

He didn't just dim my light,
He put it out.

I've learned that you shouldn't have to dim your light to appease one's ego.
You shouldn't have to lessen your value or silence your victories.
You shouldn't have to feel uneasy about wanting to celebrate yourself.
You shouldn't have to feel like you don't deserve to be confident because others might view you as cocky
Most important, you should never get the feeling that your victory, big or small, doesn't matter or it wasn't big enough to be celebrated.
Especially around people supposed to love you, care for you and want to see you do amazing things.

I'm a lover and when I care about you, I want to see you at your absolute best, your highest, your happiest and I want to be right by your side cheering you on.
That's how it should feel and that how it should be when you love someone. It's like you'd do anything to be right there when they reach their dreams or their peak because seeing them happy should bring you just as much happiness.

Yes, he put my fire out.
But I lit my shit back up and I'm shining brighter than ever now!

MANIPULATION:

PUSHING YOU AWAY BUT REFUSING TO LET YOU GO.

I tried so hard to move on.
I'd revoke all access. I'd separate myself from him. I even tried moving on with other people to take the step to move forward without him.
But *toxic people always get the urge to maneuver their way back into the toxic homes they created.*

9/10 they'll always fight like hell and somehow someway find their way back into your presence.
It's funny, isn't it? If they'd put that much of a fight to heal themselves or to keep you when they had you, you wouldn't even be in this situation right now.

He made it abundantly clear I was never going to be enough for him while also clarifying that I would not be enough for anyone else but him. It makes absolutely no sense but all the sense in the world when you've been a victim.

You don't want me. You beat me up, verbally and emotionally. You tell me I'm not enough. I leave or I leave. You chase me. You tell me I'm your everything. You tell me how sorry you are. You tell me things will change. I come back. Things start well just to revert within days. You don't want me. You beat me up, verbally and emotionally. You tell me I'm not enough. I leave or I leave. You chase me. You tell me I'm your everything. You tell me how sorry you are. You tell me things will change. I come back. Things start off well just to revert within days. You don't want me. And *the cycle continues.*

I'M SORRY, I LOVE YOU, I WANT YOU BACK, BUT I'M NOT CHANGING.

No feeling compares to someone you love coming to you, putting their pride and ego to the side and apologizing to you. It makes you feel heard, validated and understood. It makes you feel like they'd much rather lose the argument than to lose you.

But what happens when they've apologized with no changed behavior? What happens when they apologize and fight to get you back into their arms just to hurt you in several other ways? What happens when you finally realize that they only apologized to shut you up? What happens when you realize they only apologized for you to let your guard back down so they can continue to use you more? What happens when you realize that they've studied you and they've learned the perfect way to apologize by lying and manipulating you into thinking they'll change eventually?

It was all a ploy to get you right back into that never-ending cycle.

I LIKE YOU/I LOVE YOU, BUT YOU DESERVE BETTER THAN ME.

"I like you/I love you. You deserve good. You deserve better than me."

It sounds like someone saying they value you to the highest capacity and that you deserve the world. You feel like they think so highly of you. I know that's what I felt. It sounds like such a good thing, like the right steps moving forward together, and in the majority of people's minds, you believe it's a compliment when in all actuality, this is what they meant to tell you.

"Hey, you. You're amazing, you're everything good, I appreciate who you are, but I'm not interested in even attempting to reach those expectations you have set in your mind for me. I love the way you make me feel, but I'm not going to be the person I know I could be for you. I'm going to be full of disappointments for you. I just want you to be prepared because I don't find you worthy of enough to take the steps in being better to and for you."

No more excuses…

We need to put an end to making excuses for the people we love.
It not only contributes to the perception that you're tolerant of their behaviors,
But it's also a disservice to them.
See, **when we love people, we have to hold them accountable for the choices they make**, or they'll continue to make the same mistakes believing there are no repercussions for their actions.
You're contributing to them being the worst version of themselves by making excuses for them.
Hold the people you love accountable so everyone can experience the best versions of each other.

- Martine Ashley

They never stood a chance against you.
Once you'd gone through your trials and tribulations
Once you overcame every obstacle that stood in your way
Once you realized that extraordinaire that lied within you
Once you grasped your power and your strength
They never stood a chance.
At your best, your happiest, your most vulnerable and
honest, they never could stand a chance
and they never will.

\- Martine Ashley

"Maybe it's time I walk away... I just don't know how or where to begin."

Walking away will never be easy, and there will never be a right time to walk away.
So, if you're sitting there searching and waiting for that one sign to pop up and say, "it's time to walk away," you'll be waiting around forever because it's just not going to happen.

You have to determine for yourself where the line is drawn. The line needs to be a separation between what all you're okay and comfortable with handling and what you can't handle, accept or deal with. When that line gets crossed, have that self-care and self-discipline to walk away despite how you feel.

Decide.

~~*"Maybe it's time I walk away..."*~~
"I am walking away."
"I am walking away because I deserve to be loved better."
"I am walking away because I deserve to be happy."
"Although I've tolerated below the bare minimum for so long, I am making the decision today to no longer tolerate it any longer from you or myself. I am deciding to walk away, for me."

Repeat the lines. Add your own 'I am walking away because.' Make the decision that you're no longer accepting less than. Decide that you've settled for way too long and settling has lost all its rights to you from this day moving forward. It doesn't matter what you accepted before making this decision. All that matters is what you do now after making the decision.

"Maybe it's time I walk away... I just don't know how or where to begin."

It's important to walk away at the earliest signs before it gets to feel impossible to do so, but sometimes we're human. We love someone so much we don't read too much into it and we let a lot of things slide until we lose ourselves completely.

Reassurance that you're making the right decision.

Sometimes after making the decision, it's easy to want to say never mind or wanting to revert. I mean, despite how bad things are, you still love them, and that doesn't just go away because they're shitty people.

"I am making the right decision for me."
"I deserve better than what I'm receiving from you and I'm no longer okay with it therefore, I am making the right decision to walk away."
"I'm am making this decision for me."
"I deserve to smile, laugh and be genuinely happy in the arms of someone who appreciates and values me. That's not you. The best decision for me is to let us go and walk away."

Every time you think about going back. Every time you think you're thinking too much into it. Every time you get a little uncomfortable, uneasy or anxious because you know things will change. Reassure yourself that it can only get better because you've settled for the worse for so long.

"Maybe it's time I walk away... I just don't know how or where to begin."

It took constant lies, hundreds of broken promises, thousands of words to break you down slowly, and thousands more of actions leading to make you feel small. It took time with repetitive manipulative behaviors and words to reel you into this toxic relationship, and it will take time for you to get past this and feel like yourself again.

Remind yourself of the truth during these times.

You should never have to suffer for love of any kind.
You should never have to sit there and beg to be loved correctly.
You shouldn't have to negotiate for respect and to be treated decently.
You should never have to be constantly lied to and manipulated.

Love is a roller coaster. There is no blueprint for it, but when you do love someone, you shouldn't be okay with disappointing them or disrespecting them. When you love someone, you shouldn't be okay with seeing tears roll down their face, knowing you're the cause of it, and doing absolutely nothing to fix it. When you love someone, their pain is your pain, and your pain is their pain. They would never be okay with inflicting so much pain unto you because it would pain them.

"Maybe it's time I walk away... I just don't know how or where to begin."

The blame game is probably where you're headed next. You're probably telling yourself that none of this would've ever happened had you loved yourself more. You're upset you let it get this far. You hate you let yourself down. You know you're taking all the blame for yourself.

There are people in this world who refuse to take accountability for their actions. I mean, they would rather lie, laugh and get out of having to take accountability for their actions. Then there are people beaten down for so long by the people they love and have been blamed for everything under the sun that wasn't their fault. So instead of refusing to take accountability, you take all the accountability, all the blame, all to yourself.

Be kind to yourself. We've all stayed in situations longer than we should have. We've all made dumb choices we wish we could go back in time and change in a heartbeat. We've all let ourselves down, some of us more times than you can count. No one is perfect. Even the ones you think are perfect. They're not.

You can't help who you love. You can't help what you didn't know. You can't help you were lied to and manipulated. So, I need you to be kind to yourself.
Take out the word dumb, stupid, helpless, etc. out of your vocabulary and replace it with human. Because you're human and it's okay to mistakes, okay to have loved someone who didn't deserve it. It's okay because you get to wake up tomorrow and learn from it. You get to wake up tomorrow and make better choices for yourself.

"Maybe it's time I walk away... I just don't know how or where to begin."

Push yourself, but also be patient with yourself at the same time.
Again, walking away will be one of the hardest battles you face. Walking away and moving forward with it.

It's going to require a lot of self-discipline.
Revoking complete access.
Not responding to them.
Forcing yourself to do what's best for you.
Pushing yourself to make the right decisions.
Stopping yourself when you feel the need to go back.

You're the driver of your life. You decide how far this goes. You decide if you walk away or if you go back. So, I need you with every bone in your body to fight all those urges, to push yourself to get the better that you deserve.

I need you to stand up and fight for you!

Battles...

Before you consider that they were your first love, the time you've invested, all the "love" you two shared together, all the obstacles you jumped through, everything you "made it through," or anything resembling an excuse to stay.

Understand that the only reason you would even have to mention these excuses are to justify or minimize the hell that you're being put through by someone who allegedly loves you.

Life won't be perfect, and no relationship is perfect. In the end, you have to be honest with yourself, and you also have to pick your battles wisely.

Going through hell **with** the person you love fighting side by side to get to the other side.
V.S.
Going through hell **because** of the person you love while you're fighting for the both of you, alone.

- Martine Ashley

REMINDER.

Learn to take a victory lap.
We're so hard on ourselves sometimes we forget to applaud, celebrate, and give ourselves a pat on the back for how far we've come and the things we've overcome.
Big step or baby step.
Pause, acknowledge it, applaud yourself for it because it was a step!
Every step you make to becoming better, to evolve, to grow deserves to be applauded.

You can't determine what's best for someone based off what you believe, how you feel or how you'd go about it. You have your own life to make choices for. Allow the people you love to make their own choices.

- Martine Ashley

Imagine a parent forcing you to live your life a certain way because in their mind, that's what they believe is best for you.
They want you to do it this specific way or go this specific route because they've suffered through enough and the last thing they want is their child going through what they had to.
So.
They're pushing.
They're preaching.
They're forcing.
That pressure to want to make them happy and proud of you weighs heavy on your shoulders.
But you still want to be able to decide for yourself because at the end of the day, it is your life.
So, because of that, you start to bear resentment towards them.
They don't want to hurt you, make you feel small, or like you aren't good enough.
But that's the energy you feel in their presence now.
That's the energy you give off when you refuse to acknowledge that everyone may have a different opinion or to live their life on their terms.
It's not fair to put someone you love through not feeling good enough or like their voice doesn't matter, even with the purest intentions at heart.

- Martine Ashley

It's time to move on and let go of the past because it's prohibiting you from the happy and peaceful life you deserve to have.

"It's easier said than done."

Walk away from people who make you feel small or useless. They don't deserve to be loved by you.

"It's easier said than done."

What you allow is what will continue.

"It's easier said than done."

But you deserve so much better than that.

"It's easier said than done."

Anything someone says in regard to helping you move forward in whatever you're going through.

"It's easier said than done."

I want you to remove that phrase from your vocabulary.
Of course
It's easy to say go reach your goals.
It's easy to say go follow that dream of yours.
It's easy to say just walk away from someone you loved.
It's easy to say just get over them and move on already.
Of course
It's much harder to actually put the work in and do it.
But just because it's hard doesn't mean it's impossible.
And when you say that phrase enough, you use it as an excuse.
I can't reach my goals. I mean, it is easier said than done right?
I can't follow my dreams. I mean, it is easier said than done right?
I can't just walk away from someone I love. I mean, it is easier said than done right?
I can't just get over them and move on already. I mean, it is easier said than done right?
You're not even aware that you're doing it.

It keeps you sucked in.
It keeps you complacent.
It keeps you comfortable.
It's difficult. It's going to take time, healing, forgiveness, and so much more to get past it and finally feel like yourself again.
But it's possible.
It can happen.
It will happen.
You just have to believe that and work towards it.

Stop using "it's easier said than done" as an excuse to stay longer, to beat yourself up longer, to accept less than longer.

Heartbreak is grieving.

You just lost someone you thought you'd spend the rest of your life with. Yes, they're still on the earth, but they're no longer with you. Life won't ever be the same way again. The routine you shared with them that's gone, out the window. One minute you're in love, you're happy, and in the blink of an eye, everything's changed. A piece of your heart dies, and everyone grieves differently. Some people bury the piece, adapt, and continue with their lives. Other people bury the piece along with their entire heart to be cold and heartless.

Either way, you have to go through the phases.

Pain.
When heartbreak first happens, the first emotion you face, your first phase is pain. You're down, you're sad, you don't know how this could've happened, and you feel broken. Nothing anyone says clicks into your head because you never thought you'd see this day.
Allow yourself to feel pain.

Anger.
After you've been in pain, you get frustrated and angry at the person who betrayed you, who ruined everything. Sometimes you're angry with yourself because you feel like you could've done more, or you feel like maybe this is your fault. You're pissed. All you want to do is figure out why, how, and what happened.

In Denial.
After anger, you're ambushed with being in denial or making excuses for them. After time has gone by, you just miss what used to be, so you're either in denial about the situation or you make excuses. Trying to figure out a way for you to get back to that place you were before the heartbreak. You don't want to face this is over. You don't want to face that they're gone. You don't want to face that they won't be your forever, your last.

Reverting Back.
It's hard, losing someone you love and it's not because they've died but because somehow, someway your time is up with them. I have to be honest, some of us have such a hard time accepting that, so we go back. We search, we make excuses, and we go back to them. We try to stick it out as friends or just try to be there, so if they fall, they can hold on to you. 30% of people go back to the people who've hurt them, go back to relationships that broke them.

Acceptance.
After you've been sitting with this heartbreak for some time now, you slowly but surely start to accept this new normal. After all the signs point to you having to let this person go because it's over, you accept. Accepting how things are and how they will be moving forward. You accept that maybe this all happened for a reason. Certain things pop out of nowhere and you realize why what happened.

Set Back.
You've been doing so well understanding that they're gone. Learning how to live this life without them. You have great days where you feel like doors are opening everywhere for you. You feel happy again, and then there are those horrible days that feel like setbacks. Where you can't help but miss what was. You understand that it's over, but damn, there are just some days that go by where you wish it wasn't and that's okay. That's normal.

Forgiveness.
A lot of people skip this phase because it's difficult, but you can't move forward until you do. After you've learned to accept what is now, you have to focus on forgiving them and forgiving yourself. The shackle that's been placed around your ankles you will carry until you let it go and forgive. This doesn't have to happen right away. You've been hurt, so it will take time and patience. Forgive when you're ready.

Moving on.
Eventually, after more time has passed, you move forward. You move on. It doesn't hurt as bad as it once did, and things look up. New adventures, new opportunities, new people enter your life, and before you know it. You've moved on from them. You're ready for what's next.

Heartbreak is grieving.
Everyone processes it differently, but inevitably you'll find yourself face to face with each phase. Some you'll check off the list fast and some you'll struggle with. But you know you will be okay. Heartbreak isn't forever.

I can't be without you
But I can't breathe without me.
I can't dream without you,
But I can't feel without me.
I can't enjoy it without you,
But I can't feel peace without me.
I can't live without you,
But I'll die without me.

- Martine Ashley

One day, you'll be forced to face all the repercussions for choosing someone over yourself for loving someone so much you let it blind you, sacrificing yourself in the name of love. That day will be the best day of your life and you won't realize that till long past because you'll be too busy being heartbroken and devasted. That day you face those repercussions, you'll have no other option but to choose you, to love you, to fight for you, and to start all over and do right by you this time.

- Martine Ashley

The fight in you.

It's refreshing to see how much fight you have in you. You fought with your entire being to make that toxic relationship work. I mean, you would do whatever it took, right? You gave pieces of yourself away. You would've crossed oceans and ran over mountains to make it work with them. When I say refreshing, it's because even if you don't believe it or see it right now because you're in this immeasurable amount of pain, which is understandable, you are a warrior. You have this undeniable strength in you. You kept fighting even when they've shown you constantly. They weren't worth fighting for. You fought despite being pushed away, being walked on, stepped over, betrayed, etc. They shut the light out inside of you, but it didn't stop you. You were determined to love that person past all of their pain and make them seem how unconditionally you loved them. Now imagine…. Just imagine using that strength, that energy, and that fight for yourself. Imagine not giving up on you. Imagine not holding your past against you. Imagine despite how often you let yourself down, you give yourself another chance, and you keep fighting, you keep going. Imagine fighting every day to prove to yourself that you're worthy of being loved., The fight you have within yourself it makes you a warrior! Now you have to be a warrior for you.

- Martine Ashley

Loving blindly creates grounds for manipulation.
It creates room to be taken advantage of, to be used.
Love with standards, character, morals and boundaries intact.

- Martine Ashley

I understand we're not perfect.
I get we make mistakes and it's a part of life.
My mistakes resulted from me loving you blindly that I would sacrifice and compromise myself to be loved by you.
You, on the other hand, your mistakes result from you being careless, from you having nothing to lose, and from you not finding me valuable enough to do everything in your power to keep.

- Martine Ashley

"How the hell do I get back out there and love again?"

Life comes with pain. Devastating, heartbreaking, unimaginable pain, but it also comes with love, laughter, happiness, joy, contentment, peace. I know that heartbreak feeling isn't something you ever want to feel again. It's something you want to avoid at all costs, but can we take a second just to appreciate that you swore you'd never be able to get over that one person, but you did. The unbearable feeling of pain you once felt in your chest, the one that made it so hard for you to breathe at one point, it's gone. They tried to break you, tried to diminish you, tried to make you feel worthless, yet here you are, stronger than ever. You built yourself back up and kept going. I get it… I know no one wants to put themselves in a position to love someone again and get hurt again. I want you to hold on to this simple fact. Love didn't hurt you. Love didn't destroy you. Love didn't break you. Love didn't lie to you and cause you to have trust issues on top of trust issues. Love didn't break your heart. Don't ever equate love with pain and suffering, because it's not. Loving the wrong person now that that can destroy you. That can break you and give you trust issues on top of trust issues. You get back out there and love again because love wasn't the problem. Loving and falling in love with the wrong person, that was the problem.

- Martine Ashley

It's okay to choose you.

It's okay to decide that you're pouring all of your energy into yourself
It's okay to do what makes you happy and sets your soul on fire.
It's okay for your desires to not match up to the world's expectation of you.
It's okay to be selfish and put your needs and wants first.
It's okay to make choices that benefit you the most in the end.
Don't ever feel like you can't choose you.
Don't ever feel guilty for it either and I know that feeling is floating around in your mind right now.
You have every right to make sure you have what you need to present yourself to the world as the best and the happiest version of yourself.
Most important you have every right to make sure the version of you looking back in the mirror is the best and the happiest version of you that is out there.
You owe yourself that much.
You owe yourself happiness, joy, peace.
It's okay to choose you.

- Martine Ashley

You can't make someone not cheat on you.
You can't make someone be faithful and honest to you.
You can't make someone fall in love with you.
You can't make someone sit and stay with you.
You can't make someone care about you.
You can't make someone feel about you the way they once did.

Some of us, from past trauma or toxic relationships, welcome taking blame that isn't ours to take.
When you've constantly been put down and blamed for things beyond your control for so long, your mind subconsciously learns to automatically always take the blame.
So, you find yourself where something happens, and your first thoughts are, "this is my fault." "What did I just do?" "How could I have prevented this from happening to me?" "Why am I always doing this?" etc.
You have no idea how or why, but it has to be your fault, right?
Everything bad that's happened to you or around you has always been your fault.
You had something to do with it in some capacity.
That's how your brain has been wired, it's not your fault, and it's not on you.
The people who've failed you, it's their fault.
For being so cowardly that they couldn't face their shortcomings, so they blamed you instead.
There is such a thing as taking too much accountability and responsibility. There are things we have control over and then there are things we have no control over.
You could have prevented none of those up there from happening and to place that kind of blame and weight on your shoulders. It'll break you.

I need you to stop.
Stop forcing yourself to be the problem.
Stop putting the burden on you.
Stop taking all the hits and all the blows.
Stop rerouting the blame that belongs to someone else, to you.
Stop lying in the bed made for someone else.
Stop putting yourself through that pain.

I T S NOT A L W A Y S ABOUT Y O U

Sometimes it's not about you. People have so much shit going on in their lives. Fighting wars in their head, they can't quite open up about because they don't even understand it yet. Traumas they haven't even addressed, let alone healed from. Demons they can't quite figure out how to face. Karmic debts they must eventually pay for. So, it's crazy to assume that something happened specifically because of you or that it was your fault. Some of us our way too good at taking blame that isn't ours to take or carrying around baggage that isn't ours to carry when it was never about us to begin with. Sometimes it's not about you.

- Martine Ashley

"How much more do I have to go through? How much more pain am I going to have to suffer through from you? How much do I have to take? How much more do you have to put me through to decide if I'm worthy enough of earning your love? Where is the line? How much more do I have to do? How much more do I have to prove?"

Love should never have to be a challenge to see how much pain you can take being by someone's side and loving them. Love shouldn't have you wondering how much more you must suffer to get that reward of being loved back in the right way. Love should never have you begging and pleading to earn it.

A love like that isn't worth it. It's a betrayal to yourself. You don't, and you shouldn't have to suffer to be happy.

- Martine Ashley

REMINDER.

It's not your fault.
People mess up.
People hurt the people they claim to love.
People make dumb choices.
People take advantage of us.
People lie and manipulate.
It's not your fault.
It's not your blame to take.
And It's not on you.

STOP

I know what you're doing.
You're beating yourself up and overthinking relentlessly.
There's an immeasurable amount of pain in your heart that you've never felt before.
This new routine of life that doesn't include them is formulating anxiety throughout your body.
It's new, it's different and a lot of us don't adapt to change well.
So, you're trying to force your mind to forget why you're in this position right now.
You're desperately trying to convince yourself that you somehow made the wrong decision by letting them go.
You strive over time creating countless excuses to comfort your mind of guilt.
You know you shouldn't go back to them, but the only thing feels right.
It feels right at this moment, but I want you to remember how it felt when you were with them.
I want you to recall the nights you would give anything for the pain to end.
I want you to relive the moments you looked in the mirror and doubted yourself because of their words or actions.
I want you to remember the uneasy feeling you felt in their presence because despite what they told you, you knew something wasn't right.
I want you to remember the pain, the agony, the hell, the tears, the anger, and the heartbreak you felt.
I want you to remember the nights you felt so alone in their arms because you knew in every aspect besides physically, they weren't there.
This is not to hurt you by reminding you of the past.
I just want you to truly know who you're thinking about going back to.

Low moments vs allowing yourself to be abused...

I battled with this in my mind for so long.
One day I'm convincing myself that if you love someone, you have to fight.
There's going to be good days and bad days, and if you love someone, you have to remain by their side even in their lowest moments.
I struggled tremendously with defining those low moments.
Then I have days where I'm frustrated because I know love shouldn't feel this way.
I recognize there are limitations and lines that shouldn't be crossed when someone values and respects you.
I've loved you so blindly that I couldn't separate having low moments from allowing someone to use and abuse you in the name of love.

- Martine Ashley

I don’t want to win.
I want to be understood.

I have my days.
I'm on this moving forward journey, but I have my days where I stumble across these feelings that hit me like an 8-wheel truck in the middle of the night.
"What if I can't get over you?"
"What if I gave up too easily?"
"What if I didn't do enough on my end to make us work?"
"What if I'm asking for too much out of you?"
"What if with time we could reach the potential I envisioned for us?"
"What if, despite how bad we were together, it wouldn't feel right with anyone else?"
For a split second, I want to run back into your arms and try again.
Then it hits me.
You shouldn't have to make so many excuses as to why someone you love refuses to value and respect you.
You shouldn't have to take the blame for the choices someone voluntarily made knowing you'd be the cost in the end.
That's when I realized that I'd rather deal with the pain of missing you occasionally, than to be with you and feel the pain of not feeling good enough every single day.

- Martine Ashley

Fear costs you...

I stayed with you out of fear.
The fear of losing you.
The fear of being alone.
The fear of growth.
The fear of change.
As time went on, I honestly became more fearful of this being all that I receive in this lifetime.
Fearful of me settling and you being it for me forever.

Setting boundaries…

What don't you like to feel?
You don't like it when someone disrespects you because it makes you feel small?
You don't like the feeling you get when someone mistreats you because it reminds you of your past trauma?
You don't like it when people don't effectively communicate with you because it makes you feel like you're not a priority?

What are the triggers for you?
When someone lies to your face?
When someone makes you feel crazy when you're not?
When someone intentionally pushes your buttons to make you jump out of character?
When someone enters your life and your intuition is going crazy?

What requirements are a must for you?
Do you need people who value honesty, loyalty and commitment?
Do you need people who prioritize family and love?
Do you need people who understand and can be patient with your anxiety, depression, or any other mental illness?

What can I offer that I need in return?
I'm willing to commit and do all I can that doesn't require me to lose myself, dim my light, or harm myself to fight and or keep a relationship.
I need that in return.
I would never cheat despite how bad things get.
I need that in return.
I want to love without having to go through hell for it.
I need that in return.

What can you not tolerate and look past?
Cheating won't only destroy me, but it'll cause insecurities on my end I might not ever be able to recover from.
I refuse to be put through that.
Projecting your insecurities and failures on to me as if I'm your punching bag and I'm not human with emotions and feelings, I can't accept.
I refuse to be put through that.
Unwillingness to commit but wanting the perks that come with being committed is something I won't continue or accept.
I refuse to be put through that.

Setting boundaries…

These questions and answers play into how you choose the boundaries you need and set for yourself. Decide what you need, what you want, what you won't tolerate, and what it is that is worth fighting for to you. Write it down. Make a mental note. Keep it with you when new people are introduced to your life, older people find their way back into your life, or people currently in your life at the moment. If they cross that boundary that you've set. Acknowledge it and address it.

Enforce the boundaries you set. There need to consequences for people who feel comfortable crossing the boundaries you set in place for you, your peace, your happiness, your mental, physical, and emotional health. Understand that anyone who crosses those boundaries could not care less about you. I mean, when you love someone, you'll do everything to respect them, their boundaries and what you need, right? So, those same standards should be applied to you.

You deserve to be respected.
Your boundaries deserve to be respected.
You deserve to have people who genuinely care about what you need.

Let's make sure you start with yourself.

Rebuilding...

Rebuilding is horrid. Starting over from scratch just seems absurd after being beaten and broken down for so long. Emotionally, mentally, and physically you're drained. It feels endless and hopeless that you'll ever reach a place of peace. Over time I've learned that every so often, there's a beauty in rebuilding and starting over. Although you have to start over again, you get a fresh start to build a new foundation on your terms. **You decide what moves forward with you and what you're done giving your power to.** Everything you go through in life shapes you into who you are. No one denies that but imagine getting to decide what you carry around for the rest of your life and what you no longer commit your energy to. You get to choose what you agree with and what defines you—no more assigning permanent spaces in your mind to people's words, actions, or opinions. You get to take your life back on your terms and do what's best for you moving forward. I don't know about you, but it sounds a little scary but also refreshing.

You cannot control people.
You cannot control things.
You cannot control certain situations,
But you can control what you allow.
You can control who you allow,
You control for how long you allow it,
And you can control how you react.
Control what you can and make peace with what you can't.
You come to a level of great peace from within once you come to terms with that.

- Martine Ashley

Your potential as a woman...

Your potential will intimidate insecure men and your strength will scare weak men.
When you're powerful and don't even realize that yet, weak mean prey on that.
They prey on women who've struggled a little bit and have yet to realize the strength they carry.
They prey, they find, and they latch on to you.
They leach on to you, sucking you of everyone ounce of strength, courage, and power you have.
Till you're nothing more than a woman who feels she needs a man to be somebody.
Never let it get this far.
Fix your crown, hold your head high, and carry yourself like the queen you are.
It could make all the difference.

- Martine Ashley

'I don't want to be loved like this.'

"That's just it. I don't want to be loved like this. I don't want to not be able to recognize myself because I've sacrificed so much of me for you. I've never felt uglier and more insecure in my life than when I've laid in your arms. It makes me despise your existence, but this isn't just about you. I don't want to be loved like this by me, either. I'm in disgust with the way I've chosen to love me with the men I've allowed to consume my body and my time for far more than they ever deserved. I'm furious with myself for all the friends and family I let manipulate me and my kindness to the point where I became desensitized. See, I'm not proud of the person I've become. **I had much higher hopes for me and to see where I've landed is completely disheartening.** I draw the line here. This is where it ends because I don't want to be loved like this any further by me or anyone else."

- Martine Ashley

Don't grant anyone permission to make you revert you back into the person you've worked your ass off to grow from and move past.
You have all the POWER with you and the decisions you make.
Permission DENIED.
Access REVOKED.

- Martine Ashley

I don't need you…

I realized I didn't need you anymore.
It's not that I didn't love you or that the love somehow faded away.
I've just felt stronger than I ever have felt before and because of that, certain aspects of my life just became more and more clear.
I became more aware of what I needed and what was holding me down.
Over time I had created all of these reasons to stick it out and make it work with you.
I was forcing myself to want this and to fight for us.
But as I lie awake today not one of those reasons to stay came close to the one reason I needed to leave.
The need and desire to receive what I deserved and to finally be happy outweighed the love I had for you.
The stronger the need for gaining myself, my happiness, and my independency back became; the less the need for you became.

- Martine Ashley

She loved him.

She loved him with her entire soul.
But he wasn't so confident in himself.
She saw it in his lowest moments, and she would've done anything, and I mean anything, to remove all the doubt he had in his mind.
She saw him for who he was.
Someone who'd been broken by his past,
And has yet to pick those pieces up and rebuild.
He hated himself and he made her pay for it every single day.
She would've taken all of his pain away for him if she could.
While he willingly projected and inflicted all his pain onto her.
He used her as his punching bag, hoping that eventually, after he's hit her enough, he'd finally feel like he won, and he'd finally feel like someone other than the shell of a man he was.
She loved him wholeheartedly,
And he broke her.

- Martine Ashley

Give yourself the time to heal. I get it. Nothing is more frustrating than feeling like you're being held back because of the pain someone else caused you. Nothing is more annoying than still feeling sad about heartbreak or break up long after the other person has moved on. Nothing is more heartbreaking than still loving someone so much, and they don't care about you, not even a little bit. Feeling all of that pressure will make you feel like you need to rush. It makes you feel like you're not doing enough on your end to get past it. So now you're not only beating yourself up about the heartbreak, but you're beating yourself about not moving on quick enough, not getting over losing someone you love fast enough. You can't win with yourself because you never allow yourself to catch a break. You never give yourself time and you're never patient with yourself. You put a lot of time, energy, and love into trying to make it work with someone. So now to let go, move on and heal, you have to give yourself all of that time, energy and love.

Be patient with yourself.
You deserve the room to heal without limitations, without a ticking clock, or without anyone's thoughts or opinions.

Perspective...

Were you not enough for him, or were you two holding each other back?
Was he that bad, or were you both just young, dumb and immaturely in love?
Could you have fought harder for him or were you two never meant to make it?
Is it not fair or were you two just not meant to be together?

Love can be painful, devasting, heartbreaking, and so many other things. While going through those emotions of guilt, pain, and anger. Having perspective makes all the difference in the world.

Sometimes the people we love aren't the ones that were meant to permanent in your life.
Sometimes the people you'd do anything to keep don't care to fight or keep you.
Sometimes the people we feel we aren't enough for are the ones that are not worthy of all we have to offer.
Sometimes you weren't the problem, neither was the other person, and you two just weren't meant to be.

It's so easy to beat yourself up.
It's so easy to blame yourself.
It's so easy to blame everyone else.

It's harder to realize that sometimes life has other plans for you than the ones you were prepared for.

- Martine Ashley

I'm proud of you.
Whether you took a step today,
Big or small
Whether you made a decision
Important or non-important
Whether you fought back
Letting go or walking away
Whether you just came to a realization.
Happiness, peace, or you.
Whether you decided that today you'd give yourself a break from trying to be okay.
I want you to know how proud of you I am.
I want to applaud you for stepping.
I want to celebrate you.
I want to congratulate you.
I want you to understand how big it is to step in any aspect of your life.
And I'm so proud of you.

- Martine Ashley

What led us here...

'In my mind, sometimes I randomly go back to us. I try to sit back and figure out where we went wrong. You and I. Did I fail you? Did you fail me? Was there something we could've done to prevent us from ripping each other apart? Was there a specific moment where I disappointed you, or you disappointed me to the point of no return? Was this something we could've avoided? I don't do this because I miss you or I want you back. We've been down this round a couple of times, and our story always ends the same way. I do it because we ended so tragically. We destroyed each other in ways we never thought were imaginable, but at one point, we're each other's high. We would've fought wars for each other. And for us to end up how we did, and I can't seem to pinpoint where exactly what lead us here. Maybe a couple of simple small things we let slide that eventually led to bigger things that would lead to the demise of you and me. Maybe we loved each other so much it hurt... it was hurting us to love each other. I have no idea what the point of this is… It's just something that I stumble across occasionally, and it bothers my soul because I don't think I'll ever figure out what it was. What led us here...'

First, love is irreplaceable?

Nothing can compare to your first love, right?
The love, the innocence, the joy, the happiness.
It's undefeated.
Unbeatable.
No one in life with ever compares to the first people you loved outside of mommy and daddy,
Is what many people would say.
Many people will even hold on to that as an excuse to hold on a little longer, to not have to let go or to not have to move on.
But who's to say your next love won't be your greatest love?
Who's to say they love you'll receive from the next people who enter your life won't make your first love feel like a disappointment?
Who's to say your first love is even worth comparing to what true love is?
Who's to say loving yourself won't be the greatest love you get to be a part of?
Yes,
The first person you love they hold a special place in your heart, good or bad because they were the first you got to experience what love is with.
You can't replace your first love,
But now you can love harder. You can love wiser. You can love stronger because of experience, age, pain, maturity and because of growth.

- Martine Ashley

Healing is finally setting yourself free after being beaten down and tied down to your past for so long.
Healing is breaking yourself down piece by piece to discover what's causing you to run away when the tiniest bit of happiness and joy enter your environment.
Healing is gaining your power back.
Healing is having to acknowledge and relieve some of your most painful, heartbreaking, gut-wrenching memories that you'd do anything to forget.
Healing is seeing their face and not having any hatred or anger towards them anymore.
Healing is hearing a word, a name or even a song and being sucked back into a past moment in your life you try to avoid at all costs.
Healing is learning so you can do everything in your power to prevent that pain from ever entering your life again in any form.
Healing is doing your share of forgiving people who you feel deep down in your soul doesn't deserve an ounce of compassion or forgiveness for the unimaginable pain they've caused you.
Healing is trying everything in your power to stop beating yourself up over the things people said and the choices people made at the expense of you.
Healing is feeling amazing, free, happy, and at peace.
Healing is going through the gruesome journey of letting go and moving on.
Healing is doing your part and sometimes feeling like it's not enough.
Healing is doing so well for such a long time, while just for you to find yourself right back into that space, you've spent months crawling out from.
Healing is healing and having to heal again.

Healing is understanding that somethings will stick with you for the rest of your life despite how much healing you do or how much accountability take.
Healing is understanding that although some things we may never forget, some things may stick with us for the rest of our lives, but it doesn't have to be your entire life.
Healing is knowing you don't have to allow pain to dictate your life.
Healing is realizing how much power you hold within yourself.
Healing is loving yourself.
Healing is being kind to yourself.
Healing is the ugliest yet most beautiful journey you'll ever take in this life.
One minute it's bad, the next it's great.
One minute it's great, the next it's bad.
Healing understands that the goodwill always finds its way back to you, and the bad doesn't stay forever.
Healing is…
Hell, and heaven.

Why?

You feel like you need to know why, right?
You feel like you won't be able to move on till you figure out why they did what they did.
Why they hurt you.
Why they betrayed you.
Why they broke you.
Why they put you through so much pain.
Why, when they had the choice, they didn't choose you.
But telling you why will not change the pain you're feeling in your chest right now.
Telling you why doesn't change the facts staring you dead in the eyes right now.
You're forcing yourself to keep reliving the pain repeatedly when you don't have to.
You're depriving yourself of the right to move forward because you can't accept that they didn't choose you when it mattered the most.
Out of all the choices they could've made, they made the one to hurt you.
And that pain, it doesn't go away easily.
You feel like you need to know why, right?
But you don't.
You don't want to move on.
You don't want to let go just yet.
So, you're holding on. You're still making excuses for them.
You don't want to accept that someone you love so much hurt you.
But they did. They hurt you. They made their choice.
Don't give them any more power of your life to where you're waiting for them to tell you why they hurt you.
Because in the end, it all hurts the same.
Figuring out why doesn't and won't change that.

"you're never going to let this go. It's like you want to punish me forever for the things I did in the past that you said you forgave me for already."

The last thing on my mind right now is punishing you for the shit you've put me through. I promise that's not my intention. I just… I wanted you to never have done it. I wanted you to value me and what we shared that you would never risk losing me for anything or anybody. I wanted you to have never done it because I wouldn't be able to look in the mirror and stomach myself if I did to you what you did. I didn't know how hard it would be to have let it go and forget it all because every day, I'm faced with a new form of temptation and I decline. I don't think about it or second guess it because I know what we share was worth it, or I mean, what I thought we shared. I guess every day that I'm faced with temptation, I resent you a little more and more for being such a coward. I resent you for not saying no and coming home. I resent you for not coming to me if you felt our home wasn't intact or that you were so unhappy you had to look elsewhere. You say you love me, and I want to believe you with every inch of my body, but you lied. You couldn't have loved me. Love should've made you say no. Love should've reminded you what you had back home. Love was nowhere in the building when you did what you did. I don't want to punish you, believe me, I don't. I guess I'm just not as forgiving as I thought I could be about this.

Dear Diary,

Today I saw his picture and for the first time in such a long time, I saw the man I used to love. I didn't see the man who broke me, the man who disrespected me every chance he could, or the man who was okay with embarrassing me. I saw his face, and the laughs we used to share made me crack a smile—the 4-5-hour phone calls we used to have made me laugh. The texts and the inside jokes between us made me realize that although there was a lot to hate about him and the time we shared, there were also some amazing moments and memories we shared that shouldn't go unnoticed. Today it was like I couldn't hate him. I appreciated the valuable times we shared because whether I want to admit it or not, some of those moments included me being at my happiest and proudest of myself. Some of those moments were the best version of myself. **I'm tired of trying to erase chunks of my life out of my memory because he was incapable of accepting my love and reciprocating it back. I was too much for him, or hell, maybe we just weren't meant to be.** Either way, I realize that I have to learn to take the good with the bad, or I will have nothing to look back at to reminisce, to tell my daughters in the future about my life, or just to be proud of how far I've come.

From this day moving forward, I'm done hating him.

- Martine Ashley

"Let's be clear; I never asked you to do any of that for me."

That's funny because you never said no either. You took and took and took from me till I had nothing left to give anymore, and now, "you never asked me to do any of that for you?" You never asked me to do any of it, but you sure as hell enjoyed all the perks that came along with it till it didn't benefit you anymore. You didn't ask me to do any of that. Well, I never asked you to walk into my life I was living perfectly fine before you came into the picture, but you did. You walked into my life, you made me fall in love with every inch of you, and you jumped ship when it got a little too hard or when it wasn't perfect anymore when the fairy tale wasn't so happily ever after all. You never had to ask me to do any of that because, unlike you, when I said I loved you, I meant it. I showed up, and I showed out every single day, and I proved that I loved you without a doubt. I guess you can't say the same because you were never invested in us. You never gave a damn, and that's the realization that's the toughest to come to terms with.

Where you put your energy into is what you'll see more of, what you'll feel more of, and what you'll constantly play throughout your mind every day till you learn to reroute your energy.
What and where you put your energy into matters.

~~"I'm so stupid, why do I keep on making these stupid choices?"~~

"I'm human. I'm allowed to make mistakes. I'm allowed to learn from my mistakes. I'm allowed to change and grow. I am not stupid."

~~"Maybe I deserve to go through this."~~
~~"I'm not good enough."~~

"I'm flawed just like everyone else and being flawed doesn't equate to me deserving less than."

~~"Had I not been so insecure. Had I not been so annoying. Had I not been overthinking so much."~~

"My past wasn't so kind to me. I'm a work in progress."

~~"I was cheated on for a reason. It's me. Something is wrong with me."~~

"Everyone is presented with choices in this life. People's poor decisions are not a reflection of me."

~~"I hate myself."~~

"I'm angry with myself as I have the right to be. I need to work on not letting myself down again."

~~"It's me. I'm too loving. I'm too forgiving. I'm too understanding."~~

"I have a heart of gold, and I just have to learn to be cautious with who I open myself up to."

What you tell yourself matters. The way you speak to yourself matters. Stop degrading yourself. Stop beating yourself down. Stop with the harsh words and treatment to yourself.

"This relationship broke me a long time ago. How do I find myself? How do I love myself again?

To love yourself, you have to know yourself. You have to get acquainted with yourself. You have to spend time with yourself and learn yourself. I know it sounds weird because like "I've been with myself since I became myself, how exactly do I learn myself?" Everyone is different. Everyone has strengths and weaknesses, and things we love and things we hate about ourselves. Some of us have great patience, and some of us lack in that department. Some of us function better in different areas, environments and some can adapt to just about anywhere. We're all different and as we grow, we experience this thing called life, love, heartbreaks, deaths, etc. We go through trials and tribulations that make us who we are, and over time we have to relearn ourselves.

When you spend time with yourself, you see what you like and don't like, you see what you need and don't need, you see what works best for you and what doesn't, you see where you thrive and where you don't, you can discover so much about yourself if you just take the time to enjoy yourself.

- Have a dedicated time for you where you're able to be by yourself and do something that you enjoy. A time where you can just enjoy yourself. Everyone needs something just for them. Everyone needs to be someone outside of their relationship, family, etc. You have to stand on your own two feet and be who you are. Find something that sets your soul on fire. Something that when you're doing it, you're at your happiest, and peace.

- Try something new. Travel. Do something different. Switch things up. Chase an old dream. Try out a new dream. Life is so short and the last thing you ever want to do is die not having lived yet.

- Forgive yourself for the things you did. We hold on and we drain ourselves, we beat ourselves up over the things we can't change any more. Let it go. You can change nothing from the past. Forgive yourself and move forward.

- Take care of yourself. Sometimes it's just as simple as that. Get your nails done occasionally, your hair done, sometimes splurge on yourself and buy that gorgeous bag or a nice watch. 80% of feeling good is looking good. Get dolled up, dress up, remind yourself that you are beautiful, that you are handsome. Sometimes that's all it takes.

- Celebrate yourself! When you do something good or great, don't just sweep it under the rug. Don't, "it's not a big deal." Go all out, throw yourself a party. I need you to treat yourself like you're a big deal because you are whether you believe it right now or not.

I never wanted to let you go…

'I never wanted to let us go, to let you go. Do you think I wanted to have to pull, scratch, and claw myself away from you and put myself through this agony? You have no idea the stress and pain I've been under because all I ever wanted to do was love you and for you to love me, but you couldn't pull your end of the stick. I fought for us. I prayed for us. I fought more. I sacrificed, I gave, I would lose myself to gain you. I did my part. I gave every inch of myself to and for you. I breathed for you. My life was you. Despite what anyone thinks or says about that, it's the truth. You don't see those nights where I picked the phone up, wrote you a message, read it, and erased it all in disappointment because I know how this will end. You don't see those moments where something happens that makes me laugh so hard, and I automatically look to find you to tell you. You don't see the nights where I have to cry myself to sleep because the pain won't end. I want to go back to you, I want to contact you, I want to go back to who we were, But I can't. I can't do that because as much as I wanted this, and us, you've proven that you don't feel the same way. You never had that same fight for us, that same drive to make us work, and to keep me the way I did for you. **I never wanted to let you go, but you gave me no other option.'**

Don't like or love someone so much you excuse their behaviors.
Everything in this life you do, good or bad, you have consequences.
Repercussions you have to face.
And the fear of losing them shouldn't give them a pass to get away with anything that causes you pain or discomfort.

\- Martine Ashley

When to run away and never look back...

When you enter a relationship, there are sacrifices and compromises you will have to make to have a successful relationship, but when it gets to a place where you must compromise your morals, standards, or the core that makes you who you are,

Everyone has insecurities. No one on this earth is 100% happy and content with every single thing about them. That's human, that's normal, but if those insecurities interfere with you in the worst way. When those insecurities are being projected on to you and you're suffering…

Dimming your light. People will walk into your life and try to minimize your accomplishments, or make you feel like you're being or doing too much. They become the biggest party pooper with you because to them, you can do nothing right.

If you're being abused in any way. Mentally, emotionally, verbally, or physically.

People who walk into your life and slowly but alienate you. They isolate you from all of your friends and family so they can manipulate you in peace without being disturbed.

When your gut tells you to walk away, when your gut is telling you that something is wrong or when your gut is screaming, listen to it.

Runaway and never look back.

Giving your power away to someone who's hurt you.

I didn't realize it till I turned off one of my favorite songs because we heard it together, and now every time I hear it, I think about you.
And I feel forced to turn it off.
I can't even enjoy certain music because of you anymore.

I didn't realize it till I avoided certain people and places because I know it would in some shape or form remind me of you.
I can't enjoy certain friendships or places anymore because of you.
Because of the memories we shared.
You ruined them all for me.

I didn't realize it till I found myself canceling plans despite you.
I stopped enjoying myself because I felt like somehow maybe it'd hurt you if you couldn't see me just out and about, maybe you'd even question where I'm at or how I'm doing.
You made feeling and being happy feel damn near impossible for me.

I didn't realize it till I found myself angry and bitter all of the time.
I'm upset that I'm not happy. I'm in pain. Seeing other people smile, be happy, and in love, it pissed me off beyond words could ever explain because it was just me.
One minute I was happy and in love. Now I'm bitter and I'm angry, and all I see is darkness.

I hate that loving you made me lose so much of me. I hate that the fact that I loved you brought me some of the worst moments in my life. I hate that I've given you so much power over my life you dictate almost everything I do and feel now.

Do not waste your energy.
Don't waste your energy on people who can't fight off the temptation for you.
Don't waste your energy on people you have to explain all you've sacrificed for them.
Don't waste your energy on people you have to force to understand your worth.
Don't waste your energy on people who not only run when things get difficult, but they make impulsive choices that affect you in the worst way, in the end.
Don't waste your energy on people who've tried to destroy you.
Do not waste your energy.

- Martine Ashley

Pain reminds us that we're alive.
Pain reminds us that we're human.
Pain reminds us we have a heart.
Pain reminds us we have a soul.
Pain reminds us we love.
Pain reminds us that we're real.

If they were afraid to lose you
They wouldn't have gambled with you.

- Martine Ashley

You hold so much power, and you're not even aware of it because a pathetic little boy walked into your life and made you feel incompetent, small, and worthless.
Sadly, some men find dominance in destroying powerful women to prove their manhood and boost their fragile little egos.
They're frightened little boys lacking in filling grow men shoes, so they take all of that frustration and anger by seeking amazing fearful strong women.
Then they destroy them piece by piece.

So, I need you to remember this…
You are not at fault for what they lacked.
You are not at fault for loving someone and giving your all to them.
But you are responsible for protecting your peace, your energy and your space.
Allow no one, including a man, to walk into your space and make you feel less than.

- Martine Ashley

Blaming you was easier.

I blamed you for every single thing that became wrong with me and my life.
I carried so much weight on my shoulders from my traumas and my past I couldn't add yet another weight or I'd crumble.
I never really wanted to deal with the guilt I felt about constantly letting myself down, so blaming you was just easier for me.
Although you had your faults, your flaws and you contributed to my traumas, this goes far beyond just you and the pain you caused me.
But you sparked the fire in me to want to address it and try to heal from everything.
Because if I have to suffer through another "love" like you due to me avoiding my past traumas, I won't make it.

- Martine Ashley

I'd much rather be alone.

I'd rather deal with all of my past trauma that makes me feel as if I'm deserving of the mediocre love that you're providing than to be with you any longer.
I'd much rather suffer through my shit instead of collecting unprovoked and undeserving hits you constantly project on to me from the baggage you choose not to acknowledge or heal from.
I can't go through being with somebody and loving them with my entire being just to feel so alone.
I can't put myself through the hell of trying to love you past your pain just for you to add on to the traumas that I will have to heal from.
I can't disrespect myself anymore for you.
I can't beat myself down to make you feel bigger anymore.
I can't keep living miserably like this.
I can't keep feeling alone like this.
I can't believe you've gotten me to where I'd rather be and feel alone than to be loved by you for another second.

- Martine Ashley

You get to decide when enough is enough.
No one may stay where you have removed them from.
You decide when you've had enough.
You decide when you deserve better.
You decide when you stop settling.
You decide what continues in the aspects of relationships, friendships, and family.
No one gets permanent placement in your life if you don't give the say so.
It's all up to you.
You have all the power.

- Martine Ashley

You don't protect someone you love by lying to them.
You can't love someone and feel like lying to them is the best way to go about any situation.
Yes, sometimes it may feel like the right thing to do, lie to them so you don't hurt them or their feelings.
I get it.
You want to know what you do when you lie to someone you love?
You take their right to feel away because it might interfere with your selfish wants and needs from them.
You take their right to decide away because you decided what they should feel or what they should do based on the lie you told.
It's like you're telling them that they're not worthy of having options or making their own decisions.
You don't lie to the people you love because one thing about the truth, it'll always find how to resurface.
You don't lie to the people you love because you don't take their right to know the truth away.
Whatever that truth is, they deserve to know every piece of it despite the reaction you might receive from them.
When you love someone, you don't lie to them.

- Martine Ashley

Because of you or despite you…

Because of you, I'm aware of what's at stake when I
choose loving someone over loving myself.
I despise you for so many things.
The hell, the trauma, the pain.
But the one thing I have to give you credit for, although
you don't deserve it, it's showing me how bad it can get,
and how bad it can feel when you love the wrong person.
How bad it can get when you avoid addressing red flags or
simply out of fear of losing someone.
How bad it can get when you let things slide that disturb
your soul and peace.
How bad it can get when you make excuses for people's
behaviors that hurt you instead of addressing it.
You taught me how bad it gets when I give up on fighting
for the love I deserve, and I settle.
You taught me the value of standards and values.
You taught me the importance of boundaries.
Because of you, I shut down, I broke down and I was
defeated.
But despite you, I will rise, I will shine, and I won't ever
allow losing sight of myself again.

- Martine Ashley

REMINDER
Actions don't lie.
You can't misread people's actions.
They're as truthful as it gets to truth.
Them not coming home to you at night, you can't misread that.
Them treating you like crap comfortably and constantly, you can't misread that.
When you tell them this certain thing bothers you and they do it again, and again, and again, you can't misread that.
Them not making an effort, you can't misread that.
Actions DO NOT LIE.

This isn't me saying I don't love you.
This is me saying that I need to love me.
This is me saying I need me more than ever right now.
This is me saying I don't want to lose sight of me completely.
This is me saying I don't want you to overshadow me and my dreams.
I want to be somebody; I want to be somebody great.
And if I give myself up now, if I don't choose me right now, if I don't give myself some light and focus, I'll just resent you for it later.
I'm not giving up or throwing the towel in on us.
I just want to make sure that me loving you doesn't overshadow or overpower me loving me.

- Martine Ashley

My entire life I've always been afraid to lose people. I used to be so afraid to speak up what was on my mind because I never knew how someone would take it, how'd they react. I was scared of being that annoying girlfriend or friend that felt too much, needed too much or did too much. So, I shut up and I bottled everything inside.

But when I blew up, I blew up. Everything came out at once. I couldn't process one thing because there wasn't just one thing. It had been thousands of things I pushed down inside myself that piled all at once and I felt like I couldn't breathe. The way that broke me, I can't go back to that ever again.

I was so afraid to lose everyone else; that I lost myself instead. Imagine sitting, blaming yourself, pitying yourself, and hating yourself because you didn't want to confront someone who hurt you or made you feel uncomfortable.

I can't have zero say anymore with what I want, need and deserve. I can't keep telling myself to shut up every time I feel the urge to speak what's on my heart. I took every hit, every punch, and almost killed myself trying to force myself to not be me.

We all decide. I never want to force anyone to stay, leave, diminish, silence or dim their light for me like I had to do for everyone else for so long. I won't force that on anyone, but I also refuse to lessen myself or quite myself down for anyone anymore.

- Martine Ashley

Sometimes there's no going back.
We love people who cause us unimaginable pain.
There's no right person wrong/bad timing.
There's no fixing it.
There's no hope for reconciliation.
There's just the damage that's been caused, the hearts that's been broken, and traumas that's been inflicted.

- Martine Ashley

Allow the people you love to make their own choices.
How else are you ever going to know where you stand with them?
The decisions they make knowing you're at stake is the greatest way to see the "love" people claim to have for you.
Let them freely and openly be who you fell in love with,
So, you can determine if they're worth being loved by someone like you, if they deserve you, and if they've earned you.

- Martine Ashley

Dear Diary,

I've been working so hard on learning to take accountability. It's so easy to blame everyone else in the world for my problems, but I don't want to do that anymore. I've realized it's gotten me nowhere. I have to look within and figure out why I find myself in these situations, why I keep allowing people to walk in and take pieces away from me. Why I can't seem to stand firmly on my own two feet unless I'm alone. Why I choose the people who are so broken and don't want to heal. I know I'm not perfect, and I've got my own problems to heal from, but I hate feeling like I won't ever find someone to value me and understand me.

- Martine Ashley

Sometimes it's not you.
Sometimes there's absolutely nothing wrong with you or how you handled the relationship.
Often, we're just too much for certain people.
And that's not referring to expecting too much or being too much.
It just means there are people who don't want to put in a certain amount of effort.
There are people who don't want to be better versions of themselves.
There are people who don't want growth.
And it's not that you're expecting too much
It's that you're expecting it from the wrong people.

- Martine Ashley

REMINDER

If it doesn't feel right to you or for your heart, don't permit yourself to stay longer than you need to.
Eliminate the cause of that feeling now before it attaches to you, before it becomes a part of you, and before the storm, along with it comes and ruins everything you ever thought you knew.

\- Martine Ashley

I don't want to be the bigger person right now.
I know, I know.
I shouldn't allow someone to make me forget my morals and my character,
But damn, I'm tired of being the only one trying.
I'm tired of feeling like I have to patch things up with people.
I'm tired of feeling responsible for making everything right.
If they cared even half as much as I did, they should be here.
Fighting for me, fighting to get me back into their lives.
I'm tired of overplaying my role in people's lives.

- Martine Ashley

'It's not you.'

I've never felt the need to dive in and focus on myself like this before.
I've just always been so dedicated to making sure that everyone was okay or that everyone was nurtured, protected and loved by me to the fullest extent.
I don't know. Lately, I've just had this strong urge to give myself everything I give to everyone else.
For once, I want to pick me.
I want to take my life into my hands and not feel like someone is restraining me.
I want to have everything I've ever dreamed of.
And I guess I'm realizing that maybe you're just not a part of that for me.
It sucks because I love you, but I'm slowly resenting you.
Not because of anything you're doing on purpose because you've been amazing.
I can't explain it, but somehow us loving each other feels like I'm being restricted.
I want you to know that it's not you.
It's us.
I feel like **maybe we've outgrown each other; we've passed the time limit being in each other's lives, or maybe we're not one for each other.**
The last thing I ever wanted to do was hurt you, but I can't risk not getting to know and love me better out of fear.
If I've learned anything in this life you never go wrong if you're doing what's needed for you.
And although hard for me to say this, it's not you.

If I never met you,
I wouldn't be in so much pain.

If I never met you,
I would never have learned the value of putting myself first.

If I never met you,
I wouldn't have to make someone jump through hoops just to get to know me.

If I never met you,
I would've never understood the importance of setting boundaries.

If I never met you,
I wouldn't have such a bad connotation to what love is.

If I never met you,
I wouldn't have known how bad it gets when you love someone far more than you love yourself.

As much bad as you've caused, I created so much good from it all.
Glass half empty? **Glass half full!**

- Martine Ashley

I’m terrified to open my heart back up.
It’s not even about them walking in and breaking my heart.
It’s not about having to move on or let go.
It’s not even about having to start back over again with someone new.
As hard as it was to get through all of that, I managed.
I made it through.
It’s…
It’s about feeling like every time someone walks into my life, I open up to them, I love them, I allow them to see those honest, raw, and vulnerable sides of me, and they leave, they take a little piece of me.
And no matter how long it’s been or how I’ve chosen to get past it, I look in the mirror, and It’s difficult to recognize myself.
It feels like a piece of me is missing
And I’m honestly so fearful of what’ll happen when I have no pieces left in me to give to anyone else or myself.
Who will I be?

- Martine Ashley

REMINDER.
Don't rush yourself to be okay.
Don't rush yourself to get back.
It's okay to break down and fall into a million pieces.
It's okay not to want to feel better or okay right now.
You have every right to sit down, feel all your pain and sulk in it for a little while.
You have every right to be sad, not to be okay, to want to feel all those emotions in your heart.

A snake is a snake.
A scorpion is a scorpion.
Whether you remove them from their environment.
No matter how much you try to love them past who, they are.
It doesn't matter how much you nurture them, tell them that they're different, see the potential they hold to be what you see for them.

A snake will always be a snake.
A scorpion will always be a scorpion.
It's their nature. It's who they are.
Stop trying to look past that and stop trying to change who they are.
Because the only one who gets hurt in the end is you.

- Martine Ashley

I always knew of where my worth lay.
I just never had enough strength and courage to enforce it.
Until now.

- Martine Ashley

Y O U CAN'T S U R V I V E LIKE T H I S

You can't possibly survive going like this. Hoping and praying for another human being to maybe one day realize the value you hold. Pushing all your wants and needs to the side for someone who could care less about your happiness, wants or needs. Relying on someone for love and comfort when all they carry is hate and war. Trusting someone who uses the fact that you love them to benefit them when they need it but can't provide a lick of consoling or peace when you need it. You can't survive like this, no one could, and no one should ever have to.

Thank you for teaching me…

Love is a powerful thing.
What you're willing to do and sacrifice for love is terrifying.
I was willing to compromise everything I had ever known to love you and to be loved back by you.
I would've killed myself to what you wanted.
I would've given anything and everything at the drop of dime to be with you.
It's heartbreaking because I know you would've let me.
Now I know,
Now I truly understand how much power I hold when I love someone, and I can't thank you enough for that.
Because I wouldn't have realized that my love can't be given to just anyone anymore.
My love is too powerful for someone who isn't ready, for someone who isn't willing, for someone who isn't worthy.
So, thank you for teaching me how valuable my love is.

You're going to battle so many wars within your everyday life, your career, friendships, relationships, family, children, etc.
The last thing you need is to get alone time where you can finally have some peace, but you can't because you're having to battle wars within yourself.

NOTICE.

Please read.

I appreciate beyond words the love I've received for my book. All I ask is that if you post a picture of any of my books anywhere that you please tag me and give rightful recognition.

Twitter: @Spicebae_
Instagram: @ReadMartineAshleyS or @MartineAshleyS
Snapchat: @MartineAshleyS
Facebook: Martine Ashley / https://www.facebook.com/martine.ashley/

Again, thank you so much for purchasing.

L - #0291 - 261020 - C0 - 216/140/6 - PB - DID2935315